A LITTLE TASTE OF

TEXAS II

Additional Copies of A LITTLE TASTE OF TEXAS II may be obtained
by sending $6.95 plus $2.25 for mailing (Texas residents add $.54 for sales tax.)
to the following address:

A LITTLE TASTE OF TEXAS II

Barbara C. Jones
541 Doubletree Drive
Highland Village, Texas 75418

ISBN# 1-831294-19-4

Copyright © 1996, Sheryn R. Jones, Highland Village, Texas
Manufactured in China

First Printing 1996   Second Printing 1998   Third Printing 2000
Fourth Printing 2001   Fifth Printing 2004

cookbook
resources LLC

Bringing Family And Friends To The Table

541 Doubletree Drive • Highland Village, Texas 75077
972-317-0246 • 855-229-2665
cookbookresources.com

INTRODUCTION

A LITTLE TASTE OF TEXAS II is a collection of recipes that reflects the unique flavors of the vast array of natural resources in Texas. It contains 110 mouth-watering recipes that present the spice, the zest and the well-seasoned essence of the hospitality of Texas. It offers a panorama of foods with the unmistakable flavor of Texas. A cuisine that has the warm-hearted friendliness of the people of Texas. Enjoy!

Table of Contents

Appetizers..5

Breads and Brunch....................................17

Soups and Salads......................................31

Vegetables and Side Dishes......................49

Main Dishes..69

Cakes and Pies..95

Cookies and Bars.....................................111

Index 121

Appetizers

Shrimp Boat Dip

1 (8 ounce) package cream cheese, softened
½ cup mayonnaise
2 teaspoons lemon juice
2 tablespoons chili sauce

1 (8 ounce) can shrimp, drained, chopped
2 green onions, finely minced
½ teaspoon seasoned salt
Chips

Whip cream cheese, mayonnaise and lemon juice until creamy. Add chili sauce, shrimp, onions and seasoned salt and mix well. Serve with chips.

Stockyard Museum in Fort Worth is a collection of photos and memorabilia from early stockyard days.

Original Hot Cheese

1 onion, finely chopped
¼ cup (½ stick) butter
1 (10 ounce) can chopped tomatoes
  with green chilies
1 (4 ounce) can chopped green
  chilies
1 (2 pound) box processed cheese
Chips

In large saucepan combine onion and butter. Cook slowly until onion is transparent, but not brown. Add tomatoes and green chilies and green chilies and stir. Cut cheese in chunks and add to onion and tomato mixture. Heat on low until cheese melts, stirring constantly. Serve hot or at room temperature with chips.

The Texas State Capitol building in Austin is the tallest state capitol building in the U.S.

Zippy Cheese Dip

1 pound lean ground beef
½ pound hot pork sausage
1 (8 ounce) jar hot salsa

2 (16 ounce) packages cubed
   processed cheese
Chips

Brown ground beef and sausage in large skillet, stirring until it crumbles. Drain and return to skillet. Add salsa and cheese. Cook over low heat, stirring constantly until cheese melts. Serve warm with chips. (Use medium salsa if you prefer.)

Municipal Rose Garden and Museum in Tyler is a 22-acre garden that is the nation's largest rose showcase, featuring 3800 rose bushes representing nearly 500 varieties.

Snappy Chili Dip

1 pound lean ground beef
1 (15 ounce) can refried beans, drained
1 (12 ounce) jar hot salsa
1 tablespoon chili powder
1 (4 ounce) can chopped green chilies
Tortilla chips

Brown ground beef in large skillet, and drain fat. Stir in all ingredients except chips. Heat until dip is thoroughly hot, stirring constantly. Serve warm with tortilla chips.

The San Jacinto Monument near Houston is the tallest monumental column in the world. It commemorates the battle of San Jacinto assuring Texas of its independence from Mexico.

Super Spinach Dip

1 (10 ounce) package frozen
  chopped spinach, thawed
1 (9 ounce) carton plain yogurt
1 cup mayonnaise

1 (1 ounce) packet ranch dressing
  mix
½ teaspoon black pepper

Squeeze spinach very dry with several paper towels. Combine all ingredients and mix well. Serve with raw vegetables or chips.

The largest equestrian sculpture in the world is the Mustangs of Las Colinas located near Dallas-Fort Worth International Airport.

Vegetable Dip

1 (10 ounce) package frozen, chopped spinach, thawed
1 (1 ounce) packet vegetable soup mix
½ onion, finely chopped
1 rib celery, finely chopped
1 cup mayonnaise
1 cup sour cream
¼ teaspoon seasoned salt
½ teaspoon Louisiana-style hot pepper sauce, optional

Drain spinach very well by pressing out all excess water. Combine remaining ingredients and mix well. Cover and chill overnight. Serve with crackers or chips.

Texas has a land and water area of 268,580 square miles. It is as large as New York, Connecticut, Rhode Island, Massachusetts, Vermont, New Hampshire, Maine, Pennsylvania, Ohio and North Carolina.

Quick Tricks

2 (8 ounce) packages cream cheese, softened

1 (16 ounce) jar thick and chunky hot salsa

In shallow bowl mash cream cheese thoroughly with fork. Add salsa and mix with fork to blend large pieces. Serve with chips.

Great Balls of Fire

1 pound lean hot sausage
1 (10 ounce) can chopped tomatoes and green chilies

1 (16 ounce) package cubed processed cheese

Brown sausage in large skillet and drain. Add tomatoes and green chilies and mix well. Add cheese to sausage mixture. Cook on low heat stirring constantly until cheese melts. Serve hot.

Deviled Ham and Cheese Spread

1 (8 ounce) package cream cheese, softened
⅔ cup mayonnaise
½ teaspoon curry powder
½ teaspoon pepper

1 (4 ounce) jar chopped pimentos, drained
1 (3 ounce) can deviled ham, finely chopped
1 tablespoon finely minced onion

In mixing bowl combine cream cheese, mayonnaise, curry powder and pepper. Whip until fairly smooth. Add pimentos, chopped ham and onion. Mix well and chill. Serve on crackers.

Texas Ranger Hall of Fame in Waco chronicles the famed lawmen who tamed the frontier. It displays commemorate the history and heritage of Texas Rangers.

Deviled Egg Spread

3 hard-boiled eggs, mashed
1 (3 ounce) package cream cheese,
   softened
4 ounces Monterey Jack cheese,
   grated
½ cup mayonnaise
½ teaspoon prepared mustard

¼ teaspoon salt
½ teaspoon white pepper
⅓ cup finely grated chopped pecans
½ (4 ounce) can chopped green chilies

In mixing bowl combine eggs, cream cheese, Monterey Jack
cheese, mayonnaise, mustard, salt and pepper and beat well.
Add chopped pecans and green chilies and mix. Chill. Serve on
crackers.

Texas is the largest of the 48 contiguous states in the U.S.

Green Eyes

4 medium dill pickles
4 slices boiled ham

Light cream cheese, softened
Black pepper

Dry pickles with a paper towel. Lightly coat one side of ham slices with cream cheese and sprinkle a little pepper on each slice. Roll pickle up in slice of ham coated with cream cheese and pepper. Chill. Slice to serve.

Party Sausages

1 cup ketchup
1 cup plum jelly
1 tablespoon lemon juice

2 tablespoons prepared mustard
2 (5 ounce) packages tiny smoked sausages

In saucepan combine all ingredients except sausages, heat and mix well. Add sausages and simmer for 10 minutes. Use cocktail toothpicks to serve.

Crab-Dip Kick

1 (8 ounce) package cream cheese,
   softened
3 tablespoons salsa

2 tablespoons prepared horseradish
1 (6 ounce) can crabmeat, drained,
   flaked

Beat cream cheese until creamy. Add salsa and horseradish and mix well. Stir in crabmeat and chill. Serve with assorted crackers.

The largest medical complex in the world is Texas Medical Center in Houston, Texas. It includes 2 medical schools, 4 nursing schools, 14 hospitals, 55,000 employees, almost 7,000 patient beds, 37,000 parking spaces, 100 buildings with 20,000,000 square feet and 12 miles of streets on 675 acres.

Breads and Brunch

Monterey Toast

1 loaf French bread, sliced
Butter, softened
1 cup mayonnaise
½ cup grated parmesan cheese

½ onion, very finely minced
½ teaspoon worcestershire sauce
Paprika

Preheat oven to 275°. Spread bread slices completely on one side with butter and place flat on baking sheet. Mix mayonnaise, cheese, onion and worcestershire sauce. Spread mixture on buttered bread, sprinkle with paprika. Place in oven for 15 minutes, then turn heat to broil until slightly brown. Watch carefully. Serve immediately.

Texas held the first indoor rodeo in the world in 1917 in Fort Worth at the Southwestern Exposition and Fat Stock Show.

Brunch Biscuits

½ cup (1 stick) butter, melted
2 cups self-rising flour
1 (8 ounce) carton sour cream

Preheat oven to 350°. Combine all ingredients and mix well. Spoon into sprayed miniature muffin tins or shape into little round balls and place 3 balls in each miniature muffin tin. Bake for 15 minutes or until light brown.

Tip: You do not need to serve butter with these biscuits because they are rich enough without it.

The longest straight-line distance from north to south in Texas is 801 miles.

The longest straight-line distance from east to west is 773 miles.

Biscuits and Sausage Gravy

3 cups biscuit mix
¾ cup milk
Gravy:
½ pound pork sausage
¼ cup (½ stick) butter

⅓ cup flour
3¼ cups milk
½ teaspoon salt
½ teaspoon pepper

Preheat oven to 400°. Combine biscuit mix and milk. Roll dough on floured wax paper to ¾- inch thickness and cut with biscuit cutter. Place on greased baking sheet and bake for 12 to 15 minutes or until golden brown. For gravy, brown sausage in skillet. Drain and reserve 1 tablespoon drippings in skillet. Set sausage aside. Add butter to drippings and melt. Add flour and cook 1 minute, stirring constantly. Gradually add milk and cook over medium heat stirring constantly until thick. Stir in seasonings and sausage. Cook until heated, stirring constantly. Serve sausage gravy over cooked biscuits. Serves 6 to 8.

Light and Crispy Waffles

2 cups biscuit mix
1 egg

½ cup oil
1⅓ cups club soda

Preheat waffle iron. Combine all ingredients in medium mixing bowl and stir by hand. Pour just enough batter to cover waffle iron. This batter can also be used for pancakes. To have waffles for a "company weekend", bake all waffles. Freeze separately on baking sheet and place in large resealable plastic bags. To heat bake at 350° for about 10 minutes.

The first Thanksgiving in North America took place in Palo Duro Canyon in 1541 with a friar leading Coronado and his men in prayers of thanksgiving. This was 79 years before Thanksgiving at Plymouth, Massachusetts.

Cornbread

1 cup flour
1 cup yellow cornmeal
¼ cup sugar
4 teaspoons baking powder

½ teaspoon salt
2 eggs
1 cup milk
¼ cup oil

Preheat oven to 375°. Mix all ingredients. Blend well. Pour in sprayed 9 x 13 x 2-inch baking pan. Bake for 25 minutes or until light brown.

The highest point in Texas is Guadalupe Peak at 8,749 feet above sea level. Its twin peak is El Capitan at 8,085 feet above sea level. They are in Guadalupe Mountains National Park in the western-most part of Texas.

Cheese Bread

2 (6 ounce) packages biscuit mix
2 eggs, beaten
¾ cup water

2 teaspoons prepared mustard
1½ cups grated cheddar
  cheese

Preheat oven to 350°. Combine all ingredients, mix well and pour into 9 x 5 x 3-inch loaf pan. Bake 45 to 50 minutes or until light brown on top. Cool bread in pan for about 25 minutes. Remove from pan, slice and serve. It is delicious sliced and spread with a little butter and toasted. Serve with soup or stew. You could also make this batter into biscuits.

Railroad and Pioneer Museum in Temple is housed in a restored, vintage depot. It includes a retired steam engine and other railroad equipment.

Quick Quiche

½ cup biscuit mix
4 eggs, beaten
6 tablespoons (¾ stick) butter,
    melted
1½ cups half-and-half cream
½ teaspoon salt

½ teaspoon pepper
3 green onions, chopped, optional
1 (4 ounce) can chopped green
    chilies
1 cup grated cheddar cheese
1 cup chopped ham

Preheat oven to 350°. In mixing bowl combine biscuit mix, eggs
and melted butter. Add remaining ingredients and mix well.
Pour in greased 10-inch pie pan or deep dish pie pan. Bake
40 minutes. Let sit at room temperature 10 minutes before serving.
Slice in wedges and serve. Serves 6 to 8.

*Texas has the largest State Fair in the U.S. and the largest
ferris wheel in North America.*

Quesadilla Pie

1 (4 ounce) can chopped green
  chilies
½ pound sausage, cooked
2 cups grated cheddar cheese

3 eggs, well beaten
1½ cups milk
¾ cup biscuit mix
Hot salsa

Preheat oven to 350°. Spray 9-inch pie pan with vegetable spray. Sprinkle green chilies in pie pan. Cook sausage, add cheese until it melts and place in pie pan over green chilies. In separate bowl, mix eggs, milk and biscuit mix. Pour over chilies, sausage and cheese. Bake for 30 minutes. Serve with salsa on top of each slice. Serves 6.

Texas is the largest oil producer in the U.S.

Breakfast Bake

1 pound hot sausage, crumbled,
    cooked
2 tablespoons dried onion flakes
1 cup grated cheddar cheese
1 cup biscuit mix
¼ teaspoon salt

¼ teaspoon pepper
4 eggs, well beaten
2 cups milk
1 (8 ounce) can whole kernel corn,
    drained, optional

Preheat oven to 350°. Place sausage in sprayed 9 x 13 x 2-inch glass baking dish. Sprinkle with onion and cheese. In mixing bowl combine biscuit mix, salt, pepper and eggs. Beat well. Add milk and stir until well blended. (If you are using this for breakfast leave out the corn, add corn if you are serving it for brunch.) Pour over sausage mixture. Bake covered for 35 minutes. (If made a day ahead, add an extra 5 minutes to cooking time since you will be taking it out of refrigerator.) Wonderful breakfast for company weekends! Serve with toast or biscuits and jelly. Serves 8.

Maple-Spice Muffins

1¼ cups flour
1½ cups whole wheat flour
½ cup quick-cooking oats
1 teaspoon baking soda
2 teaspoons baking powder
2 teaspoons cinnamon
½ teaspoon ground cloves
2 eggs
1 (8 ounce) carton sour cream
1 cup maple syrup
1 cup firmly packed brown sugar
½ cup oil
½ teaspoon maple flavoring
1 banana, mashed
1 cup chopped walnuts

Preheat oven to 375°. In mixing bowl combine flours, oats, baking soda, baking powder, cinnamon and cloves and mix well. Add eggs, sour cream, maple syrup, brown sugar, oil, maple flavoring and mashed banana. Stir well by hand. Add walnuts and pour into 24 paper-lined muffin tins. Bake for 18 to 20 minutes.

Best Bran Muffins

½ cup rolled oats
1 cup white flour
1 cup whole wheat flour
½ cup Bran Buds
½ teaspoon salt
1 teaspoon baking powder
1 teaspoon baking soda
⅔ cup sugar
1½ teaspoons cinnamon
1 egg, beaten
¼ cup oil
½ cup corn syrup
¾ cup buttermilk
1 (8 ounce) can crushed pineapple
    with juice
½ cup chopped pecans

Preheat oven to 375°. In mixing bowl combine oats, flours, bran, salt, baking powder, baking soda, sugar and cinnamon. Make a well in center and add egg, oil, corn syrup and buttermilk. Mix well. Stir in pineapple and pecans. Fill 18 to 20 muffin cups ⅔ full. Bake for 14 to 15 minutes or until golden brown.

Grand Kid's Special

4 slices white bread, crusts trimmed
Peanut butter
Grape or plum jelly
2 eggs, well beaten
Butter
Powdered sugar
Maple syrup

Spread peanut butter and jelly on 2 slices of bread. Top with remaining 2 slices of bread. Beat eggs in shallow bowl. Dip each sandwich in egg. Melt about 2 tablespoons of butter in skillet and cook each sandwich on both sides until light brown. Remove from skillet and sprinkle lightly with powdered sugar. Serve with maple syrup.

The world's biggest oil gusher was Spindletop near Beaumont in 1901. The gusher blew more than 100 feet in the air and spewed more than 100,000 gallons of oil per day for 9 days before it was capped.

Treasure-Filled Apples

6 medium, tart apples
½ cup sugar

¼ cup red hot candies
¼ teaspoon ground cinnamon

Preheat oven to 350°. Cut tops off apples and set tops aside. Core apple to within ½-inch of bottom. Place in greased 8-inch of bottom. Place in candies and cinnamon and spoon 2 tablespoons into each apple. Replace tops. Spoon any remaining sugar mixture over apples. Bake uncovered for 30 to 35 minutes or until apples are tender. Baste occasionally.

The largest natural gas field in the world is located north of Amarillo and is called Panhandle-Hugoton Field. It is estimated that the field contains more than 25 trillion cubic feet of gas and has produced over 8 trillion since its discovery in 1918.

Soups
and
Salads

Incredible Broccoli-Cheese Soup

1 (10 ounce) box frozen chopped
    broccoli
3 tablespoons (⅓ stick) butter
½ onion, finely chopped
¼ cup flour
1 (16 ounce) carton half-and-half
    cream
1 (14 ounce) can chicken broth

½ teaspoon salt
¼ teaspoon black pepper
⅛ teaspoon cayenne pepper
½ teaspoon summer savory
½ (16 ounce) package cubed,
    mild Mexican processed
    cheese

Punch several holes in box of broccoli and microwave for
5 minutes. Turn box in microwave and cook another 4 minutes.
Leave in microwave for 3 minutes. In large saucepan melt butter
and saute onion, but do not brown. Add flour and stir, gradually
add half-and-half, chicken broth and seasonings, stirring constantly.
Heat until mixture thickens. Do not boil. Add cheese and heat
until cheese melts, stirring constantly. Add cooked broccoli.
Serve hot. Serves 4 to 6.

Taco Soup

- 1½ pounds lean ground beef
- 1 onion, chopped
- 1 (1.5 ounce) packet taco seasoning
- 1 (15 ounce) whole kernel corn with liquid
- 1 (15 ounce) can pinto beans with liquid
- 1 (14 ounce) can Mexican seasoned tomatoes with liquid
- 1 cup water
- 1 (14 ounce) can beef broth
- Sour cream for garnish

In large roasting pan brown beef and chopped onion and stir well. Add taco seasoning, corn, beans, tomatoes, water and broth and stir well. Bring to boiling point, turn heat down and simmer for 2 hours. Ladle soup in bowls and garnish with dollop of sour cream. Serve with tortilla chips. Serves 8.

Tip: May be cooked in slow cooker all day.

Cream of Zucchini Soup

1 small onion, finely chopped
2 tablespoons butter
3½ cups unpeeled, grated zucchini
1 (14 ounce) can chicken broth

1 teaspoon seasoned salt
1 teaspoon dill weed
½ teaspoon white pepper
1 (8 ounce) carton sour cream

In saucepan saute onion in butter until onion is lightly cooked, but not brown. Add zucchini, broth, seasoned salt, dill weed and pepper and bring to boiling point. Turn heat to low and simmer 15 minutes. Stir in sour cream and mix well. Bring to boiling point, but do not boil. Remove from heat and serve. Serves 4 to 8.

Pecos is the home of the luscious cantaloupe that is the delight of gourmets throughout the United States. Grown in irrigated fields, the quality derives from the natural combination of alkali soil, Texas sunlight and altitude.

White Lightning Chili

- 1½ cups dried navy beans
- 3 (14 ounce) cans chicken broth
- 2 tablespoons (¼ stick) butter
- 1 cup water
- 1 onion, chopped
- 1 clove garlic, minced
- 3 cups chopped, cooked chicken
- 1 (4 ounce) can chopped green chilies
- ½ teaspoon sweet basil
- ½ teaspoon white pepper
- 1½ teaspoons ground cumin
- ½ teaspoon dried oregano
- ⅛ teaspoon cayenne pepper
- ⅛ teaspoon ground cloves
- Grated Monterey Jack cheese

Sort and wash beans and place in a large stockpot. Cover with 2 inches of water. Soak overnight. Drain beans. Add broth, butter, water, onion and garlic. Bring to boil, reduce heat and cover. Simmer 2 hours, stirring occasionally, add boiling water as needed. Mash beans with a potato masher several times until half the beans are mashed. Add chicken, green chilies and seasonings. Bring to boil, reduce heat and cover. Simmer 30 minutes. When ready to serve, spoon in bowls and top with a tablespoon or two of cheese. Serves 8.

Cauliflower Salad

¾ cup sour cream
1 cup mayonnaise
1 (1 ounce) packet ranch dressing
    mix
1 large head cauliflower, broken into
    bite-size pieces
3 ribs celery, sliced
1 bunch green onions with tops,
    chopped

1 (8 ounce) can water chestnuts,
    drained
⅓ cup sweet relish, drained
1 (8 ounce) package shredded
    Monterey Jack cheese
1 (10 ounce) package frozen
    green peas, thawed, drained,
    uncooked
1 (2.25 ounce) package sliced
    almonds

Mix sour cream, mayonnaise and dressing and put aside. In large
plastic container with lid combine the well-drained cauliflower,
celery, green onions, water chestnuts, relish, cheese, peas and
almonds. Add dressing, cover and toss. Serve in crystal bowl.
Serves 10 to 12.

Crunchy Broccoli Salad

- 1 bunch fresh broccoli, washed, well drained
- 1 bunch green onions with tops, chopped
- 4 hard-boiled eggs, sliced
- 1 (8 ounce) can sliced water chestnuts, drained
- 1 (14 ounce) can bean sprouts, drained
- 1 (2.5 ounce) package slivered almonds
- 1 (1 ounce) packet ranch salad dressing mix
- 1 cup mayonnaise

Cut broccoli in small bite-size pieces and make sure broccoli drains completely. (It is a good idea to wash and drain broccoli 1 day earlier and place in plastic bag with a couple of paper towels to help soak up moisture.) Mix broccoli, onions, eggs, water chestnuts, bean sprouts and almonds in large mixing bowl. In small bowl mix ranch dressing with mayonnaise and add to broccoli mixture. Toss and chill. Serves 8.

Black-Eyed Pea Salad

2 (16 ounce) cans jalapeno black-
    eyed peas, rinsed, drained
1 ripe avocado, peeled, chopped
½ purple onion, chopped
¾ cup fresh sliced mushrooms
1 (4 ounce) can chopped green
    chilies
1 (4 ounce) can ripe olives, chopped
1 green bell pepper, seeded,
    chopped

Dressing:
⅓ cup oil
⅓ cup white wine vinegar
3 tablespoons sugar
1 tablespoon dried parsley
    flakes
¼ teaspoon garlic powder
1 teaspoon seasoned salt
½ teaspoon pepper
1 teaspoon salt

In large bowl mix black-eyed peas, avocado, onions, mushrooms,
green chilies, olives and bell pepper. Mix dressing ingredients in
small bowl. Add dressing to vegetables and toss. Chill. Serves 10.

Cornbread Salad

- 2 (6 ounce) packages Mexican cornbread mix
- 2 eggs
- 1⅓ cups milk
- 2 ribs celery, sliced
- 1 bunch green onion with tops, chopped
- 1 green bell pepper, chopped
- 2 tomatoes, chopped, drained
- 8 slices bacon, cooked, crumbled
- 1 (8 ounce) package grated cheddar cheese
- 1 (8 ounce) can whole kernel corn, drained
- ½ cup ripe chopped olives
- 2½ cups mayonnaise

Prepare cornbread according to package directions with egg and milk. Cook, cool and crumble cornbread in large mixing bowl. Add celery, green onions, bell pepper, tomatoes, bacon, cheese, corn, olives and mayonnaise and toss. Chill several hours and serve.

Belton Lake is a scenic 12,300–acre impoundment of the Leon River and several creeks.

Waldorf Salad Supreme

1 tablespoon lemon juice
3 unpeeled, apples, coarsely
   chopped
3 ribs celery, chopped
1 cup green grapes, halved

1 (16 ounce) can pineapple
   chunks, drained
¾ cup pecan halves
⅔ cup mayonnaise
Lettuce

In large bowl pour lemon juice over apples and toss. Add celery, green grapes, pineapple, pecan halves and mayonnaise. Toss. Serve on lettuce leaf. Serves 6.

Morton H. Meyerson Symphony Center in Dallas is a multi-million dollar facility designed by architect I. M. Pei. It is the 260,000-square foot home of the Dallas Symphony Orchestra.

Cucumbers in Sour Cream

2 cucumbers, peeled, sliced
1 (8 ounce) carton sour cream
½ onion, very finely minced
2 tablespoons lemon juice
1 teaspoon salt
1 tablespoon sugar

Put cucumbers in a bowl. Combine remaining ingredients and pour over cucumbers. Cover and chill.

Cherry-Cranberry Salad

1 (6 ounce) package cherry gelatin
1 cup boiling water
1 (20 ounce) can cherry pie filling
1 (16 ounce) can whole cranberry sauce

In large bowl combine cherry gelatin and boiling water, mix until gelatin dissolves. Add pie filling and cranberry sauce. Pour in 7 x 11 x 2-inch dish and refrigerate. Serve on lettuce leaf. Serves 6 to 8.

Piña Colada Salad

1 (12 ounce) carton small-curd
  cottage cheese
1 (6 ounce) package lemon gelatin
1 (15 ounce) crushed pineapple,
  drained

1 (3½ ounce) can flaked coconut
½ teaspoon coconut extract
½ teaspoon pineapple extract
1 (8 ounce) carton whipped cream

In large bowl combine cottage cheese and dry lemon gelatin and
mix well. Add pineapple, coconut and extracts. Fold in whipped
cream. Chill. Serve in crystal bowl. Serves 8.

*Texas Children's Hospital is the largest freestanding
hospital in the U.S. and is part of the Texas Medical
Center in Houston.*

Creamy Fruit Salad

1 (12 ounce) can sweetened condensed milk
¼ cup lemon juice
1 (20 ounce) can peach pie filling*
1 (15 ounce) can pineapple chunks, drained
2 (15 ounce) cans fruit cocktail, drained
1 cup chopped pecans
1 (8 ounce) carton whipped topping

In large bowl combine condensed milk and lemon juice. Stir until well blended. Add pie filling, pineapple chunks, fruit cocktail and pecans and mix. Fold in whipped topping. Serve in crystal bowl. Serves 12 to 14.

*You may substitute any other pie filling.

Fort Hood in Killeen covers 339 square miles and is staffed with the largest collection of soldiers and fighting machines in the free world.

Orange-Fluff Salad

1 (15 ounce) can crushed pineapple
   with liquid
1 (6 ounce) package orange gelatin
1 (8 ounce) can mandarin oranges,
   drained
2 cups buttermilk
1 (8 ounce) carton
   whipped topping
1 cup chopped pecans
Lettuce leaves

In large saucepan bring pineapple and its liquid to boil. Remove from heat and stir in gelatin. Stir until gelatin dissolves. Add mandarin oranges and cool. Add buttermilk to pineapple mixture and chill until consistence of unbeaten egg white. Fold in whipped topping and pecans. Spoon mixture into lightly greased 9 x 13 x 2-inch glass dish. Chill several hours before serving. Cut in squares and serve on lettuce leaf. This makes a nice "light" salad. Serves 12.

Incredible Strawberry Salad

2 (8 ounce) packages cream cheese, softened
2 tablespoons mayonnaise
½ cup powdered sugar
1 (16 ounce) package frozen strawberries, thawed
1 cup miniature marshmallows
1 (8 ounce) can crushed pineapple, drained
1 (8 ounce) carton whipped topping
1 cup chopped pecans

In large mixing bowl combine cream cheese, mayonnaise and powdered sugar. Beat until creamy. Fold into strawberries (if strawberries are large, cut them in half), marshmallows, pineapple, whipped topping and pecans. Pour in 9 x 13 x 2-inch glass dish. Freeze. Remove from freezer about 15 minutes before cutting and serving. Serves 12.

Shrimp and English Pea Salad

2 cups frozen shrimp, thawed, cooked, cleaned
1 (10 ounce) package frozen green peas, thawed, uncooked
2 ribs celery, chopped
1 cup mayonnaise
⅓ cup pickle relish, drained
1 tablespoon lemon juice
½ teaspoon curry powder
½ teaspoon pepper
¼ teaspoon salt
1 (3 ounce) can chow mein noodles
1 cup chopped cashews
Lettuce leaves

Blot shrimp with paper towels and make sure all liquid absorbs. Combine shrimp, peas, celery, mayonnaise, relish, lemon juice, curry powder, pepper and salt in large bowl. Toss. Cover and chill at least 1 hour. Before serving, add noodles and cashews and toss. Serve on lettuce leaves. Serves 8.

Dallas Museum of Art has a superb collection of pre-Columbian artwork plus major European and American Art.

Ginger-Shrimp Pasta Salad

5 ounces uncooked vermicelli
2½ cups cooked shrimp
1 (8 ounce) can water chestnuts
1 tablespoon dried parsley
1 carrot, shredded
½ cup frozen peas, thawed, uncooked
Lettuce

Ginger Dressing:
½ cup mayonnaise
⅓ cup sour cream
1 tablespoon soy sauce
1 teaspoon sugar
½ teaspoon seasoned salt
¾ teaspoon powdered ginger
⅛ teaspoon red pepper

Break vermicelli in small pieces. Cook as directed on package and drain. Rinse in cold water and drain very well. Combine vermicelli, shrimp, water chestnuts, parsley, carrot and green peas. Combine all dressing ingredients, pour over salad and toss. Serve on a lettuce leaf. Serves 8.

Angel Salad

1 (8 ounce) package cream cheese,
    softened
½ cup sugar
1 (16 ounce) can chunky fruit
    cocktail, drained

1 (15 ounce) can pineapple
    chunks, drained
1 (8 ounce) carton whipped
    topping

Beat cream cheese and sugar with mixer until creamy. Add fruit and mix gently. Fold in whipped topping, pour into crystal bowl and chill.

The first corny dog was made by Neil Fletcher in his kitchen in the 1940's. The corny dog was served at the State Fair of Texas and it became popular mealtime treat nationwide.

Vegetables and Side Dishes

Baked Cauliflower

1 (16 ounce) package frozen
　cauliflower
1 egg
⅔ cup mayonnaise
1 (10 ounce) can cream of chicken
　soup
1 cup grated cheddar cheese

2 ribs celery, sliced
1 bell pepper, seeded, chopped
1 onion, chopped
1 teaspoon black pepper
1 cup cracker crumbs
Paprika

Preheat oven to 350°. Place cauliflower in sprayed 9 x 13-inch glass baking dish and cover with plastic wrap leaving one corner open. Cook in high in microwave for 3 minutes. Turn pan and cook another 3 minutes on high. In medium saucepan, combine egg, mayonnaise, chicken soup and cheese. Heat just until well mixed. Add celery, bell pepper, onion and black pepper to cauliflower and mix well. Pour soup mixture over vegetables and spread evenly. Sprinkle cracker crumbs on top. Bake 35 to 40 minutes. Sprinkle paprika over top of casserole before serving. Serves 10 to 12.

Zippy Zucchini

4 eggs
1 (16 ounce) package shredded Monterey Jack cheese
1 (8 ounce) package shredded cheddar cheese
4 cups zucchini
1 (4 ounce) can chopped green chilies
1 (2 ounce) jar sliced pimentos
1 onion, finely chopped
1 teaspoon seasoned salt
⅛ teaspoon cayenne pepper
1 cup crushed croutons
⅓ cup grated parmesan cheese

Preheat oven to 350°. In large mixing bowl beat eggs well. Mix in Monterey Jack and cheddar cheeses, zucchini, green chilies, pimentos, onion, seasoned salt and cayenne pepper and mix well. Pour in well greased 2-quart baking dish. Mix croutons and parmesan cheese, sprinkle over vegetables and bake uncovered for 35 minutes. Serves 8.

The Ameriquest Field in Arlington is the home of the American League Texas Rangers.

Posh Squash

8 medium yellow squash, sliced
1 onion, chopped

½ (16 ounce) package cubed
Mexican processed cheese

Preheat oven to 350°. Cook squash and onion until tender. Drain and add cheese and stir over low heat until cheese melts. Pour in sprayed 2-quart baking dish and bake 15 minutes.

Creamy Squash

8 medium yellow squash
1 (8 ounce) package cream cheese,
    softened

Salt and pepper

Cook squash until tender. Drain. Dice cream cheese and add to squash. Add salt and pepper. Cook on low heat, stirring constantly until cream cheese melts. Serve hot.

Squash Dressing

- 2 (6 ounce) packages Mexican cornbread mix
- 2 eggs
- 1⅓ cups milk
- 2 pounds yellow squash, sliced
- 1 cup water
- ½ cup (1 stick) butter
- 1 cup chopped onion
- 1 cup chopped celery
- ½ cup chopped green bell pepper
- 1 (10 ounce) can cream of chicken soup, undiluted
- 2 cups milk
- 2 teaspoons poultry seasoning

Preheat oven to 350°. Prepare and bake cornbread according to package directions. Cool and crumble in large bowl. Combine squash and water in saucepan and bring to boil. Cook about 8 minutes until squash is tender. Drain and mash. Melt butter in skillet over medium heat and saute onion, celery and bell pepper. Combine crumbled cornbread, squash, onion mixture, cream of chicken soup, milk and poultry seasoning. Mix well and spoon into sprayed 9 x 13 x 2-inch glass baking dish. Bake for 45 minutes. Serves 10 to 12.

Shoe-Peg Corn

¼ cup (½ stick) butter
1 (8 ounce) package cream cheese
3 (16 ounce) cans shoe-peg corn, drained
1 (4 ounce) can chopped green chilies

2 ribs celery, sliced
1 bell pepper, chopped
½ teaspoon seasoned salt
½ teaspoon white pepper
1½ cups crushed cracker crumbs

Melt butter in large saucepan and stir in cream cheese. Heat on low until cream cheese melts and blends well. Add corn, green chilies, celery, bell pepper, salt and pepper. Mix and pour into greased 9 x 13 x 2-inch baking dish. Sprinkle cracker crumbs over casserole and bake for 30 minutes. Serves 10.

Lyndon B. Johnson Lake, a 14,440-acre reservoir, is among Texas' most popular outdoor recreation destinations for swimmers, scuba divers, boaters and fishermen.

Spinach Special

- 2 (10 ounce) packages frozen, chopped spinach
- 1 (16 ounce) carton small curd cottage cheese
- 2½ cups grated cheddar cheese
- 4 eggs, beaten
- 3 tablespoons flour
- 4 tablespoons (½ stick) butter
- ¼ teaspoon garlic salt
- ½ teaspoon lemon pepper
- ¼ teaspoon celery salt
- 1 tablespoon dried onion flakes

Defrost spinach and squeeze out all water. In large bowl mix all ingredients. Pour into sprayed 2½-quart baking dish. Bake for 1 hour. Serves 8.

Tip: Casserole may be made a day ahead and baked when ready to serve.

The Lyndon B. Johnson boyhood home is in Johnson City.

Jalapeño Green Beans

3 (15 ounce) cans green beans
1 (8 ounce) carton sour cream
½ (1 pound) box jalapeno processed
  cheese, diced

1 onion, finely minced
2 cups crushed crispy rice cereal or
  corn flakes
4 tablespoons (¼ stick) butter

Drain green beans. In large saucepan on low heat melt sour cream and cheese, stirring constantly. Add onion and green beans and mix well. Pour into sprayed 9 x 13 x 2-inch baking dish. Combine crushed cereal and butter and sprinkle over green bean mixture and bake for 35 minutes at 325°. Serves 10 to 12.

Lake Texoma is a huge reservoir of over 88,000-acres impounding Red River. It is one of the most popular Corps of Engineers' lakes in the nation.

Scalloped Corn and Tomatoes

2 (15 ounce) cans Mexican seasoned tomatoes with liquid
1 (15 ounce) can whole kernel corn, drained
1 (15 ounce) can cream-style corn
½ cup (1 stick) butter, melted, divided
½ cup grated cheddar cheese
1 onion, chopped
2 tablespoons cornstarch
2 eggs, beaten
2 teaspoons sugar
½ teaspoon seasoned salt
½ to 1 teaspoon pepper
¼ teaspoon garlic powder
1½ cups cracker crumbs
½ cup parmesan cheese

Preheat oven to 350°. In large bowl mix tomatoes, both cans of corn, butter, cheese, onion, cornstarch, eggs, sugar and seasonings. Pour into sprayed 9 x 13 x 2-inch baking dish. In small bowl mix crumbs, butter and parmesan cheese. Sprinkle over top of casserole. Bake uncovered for 50 minutes. Serves 10 to 12.

Broccoli Supreme

2 (10 ounce) packages frozen
    broccoli spears, thawed
3 tablespoons butter
3 tablespoons flour
¾ teaspoon salt
⅛ teaspoon paprika

¼ teaspoon black pepper
1⅔ cups milk
1 (8 ounce) package shredded
    cheddar cheese
1 (5 ounce) can cashews

Cook broccoli by microwave instructions on package. Place
broccoli in 2-quart baking dish. In saucepan melt butter, add flour,
salt, paprika and black pepper. Stir well. Over medium heat add
milk, stirring constantly until sauce is smooth and thick. Add
grated cheese and cashews. Heat and mix well. Pour sauce over
broccoli and serve. Serves 8 to 10.

With more than 30 structures that bear State Historical
Medallions, Jefferson is one of the most historic towns in
Texas.

Mexican Mac

1 cup cut macaroni, uncooked
1 (15 ounce) can Mexican seasoned tomatoes with liquid
1 (10 ounce) can cream of mushroom soup, undiluted
1 (8 ounce) carton sour cream
1 (4 ounce) can chopped green chilies
1 (8 ounce) package shredded Monterey Jack cheese
½ teaspoon seasoned salt
⅛ teaspoon cayenne pepper, optional
1½ cups shredded cheddar cheese

Preheat oven to 350°. Cook macaroni according to directions and drain. Combine all ingredients except cheddar cheese. Pour in sprayed 9 x 13 x 2-inch baking dish. Top with cheddar cheese. Bake covered for 35 minutes. Serves 10 to 12.

Tyler, Texas is known as the "Rose Capital of the World".

Ranch Beans

1 pound uncooked, dried pinto
    beans
3 quarts water
¼ pound bacon
1 onion, chopped

1 teaspoon garlic powder
2 teaspoons chili powder
½ teaspoon dried oregano
1 teaspoon cumin
1 teaspoon salt

Sort and wash beans. Place beans in large saucepan and add enough water to cover beans by about 2 inches. Soak overnight or bring to boil for 2 minutes. Remove from heat and let soak for 1 hour. Drain. Add 3 quarts water and bring to boil. Cook bacon in skillet until crisp. Dice bacon and add to beans plus 2 tablespoons of drippings. Add onion, garlic powder, chili powder, oregano and cumin. Cook for 2 to 3 hours or until beans are tender. If beans become dry add boiling water. Season with salt when they are done. Serves 12.

Mashed Potatoes

8 medium to large potatoes
1 (8 ounce) carton sour cream
1 (8 ounce) package cream cheese, softened
1 teaspoon salt
½ teaspoon white pepper
Butter

Preheat oven to 325°. Peel, cut up and boil potatoes. Drain. Whip hot potatoes and add sour cream, cream cheese, salt and pepper. Continue whipping until cream cheese melts. Pour in sprayed 3-quart baking dish. Dot generously with butter. Cover with foil and bake for 20 minutes. Add 10 minutes cooking time if you are reheating them. Serves 8.

Tip: This can be made the day before and reheated.

Jay Gould Private Railroad car in Jefferson has a luxurious interior with four staterooms, lounge, dining room, kitchen, butler's pantry and bathroom.

Cheddar-Potato Casserole

1 (32 ounce) bag frozen hash brown
    potatoes, thawed
1 onion, chopped
¾ cup (1¼ sticks) butter, melted,
    divided

1 (8 ounce) carton sour cream
1 (10 ounce) can cream of
    chicken soup, undiluted
1 (16 ounce) package shredded
    cheddar cheese
1½ cups crushed corn flakes

Preheat oven to 350°. In large mixing bowl combine hash brown
potatoes, onion, ½ cup melted butter, sour cream, soup and cheese.
Mix well. Pour in greased 9 x 13 x 2-inch baking dish. Combine
corn flakes with 2 tablespoons melted butter and sprinkle over
casserole. Bake for 50 minutes. Serves 12.

Scalloped Potatoes

6 medium potatoes
½ cup (1 stick) butter, divided
Black pepper
1 tablespoon flour

1 (16 ounce) package shredded cheddar cheese, divided
¾ cup milk

Preheat oven to 350°. Peel, wash potatoes and slice half of potatoes and place in 3-quart sprayed baking dish. Slice butter and place half over potatoes. Sprinkle with pepper. Sprinkle flour over top of pepper. Cover with half the cheese. Slice remaining potatoes and place over first layer and add remaining butter slices. Pour milk over casserole and sprinkle a little more pepper. Top with remaining cheese. Cover and bake for 1 hour. (This must be cooked immediately or potatoes will darken.) It can be frozen after baking and reheated. Serves 8.

Sweet Potato Casserole

1 (29 ounce) can sweet potatoes, drained
⅓ cup evaporated milk
¾ cup sugar
2 eggs, beaten
¼ cup (½ stick) butter, melted

1 teaspoon vanilla extract
Topping:
1 cup packed light brown sugar
3 tablespoons (⅓ stick) butter, melted
½ cup flour
1 cup chopped pecans

Preheat oven to 350°. Place sweet potatoes in mixing bowl and mash slightly with fork. Add evaporated milk, sugar, eggs, butter and vanilla. Mix well. Pour in greased 7 x 11 x 2-inch baking dish. Mix topping ingredients and sprinkle over top of casserole. Bake uncovered 35 minutes or until top is crusty. Serves 8.

Puddin' Hill Bakery in Greenville offers a scrumptious array of world famous pecan fruit cakes and chocolate delicacies.

Texas Rice

- 1 onion, chopped
- ¼ cup (½ stick) butter
- 4 cups cooked white rice (use instant rice)
- 2 (8 ounce) cartons sour cream
- 1 cup cream-style cottage cheese
- ¾ teaspoon seasoned salt
- ¼ teaspoon white pepper
- 1 (4 ounce) can chopped green chilies
- 1 (16 ounce) package shredded cheddar cheese, divided

Preheat oven to 350°. In large saucepan saute onion in butter until clear. Remove from heat, stir in rice, sour cream, cottage cheese, seasoned salt and pepper. Toss lightly to mix well. Place half rice mixture in sprayed 9 x 13 x 2-inch baking dish and sprinkle the green chilies over mixture. Sprinkle half the cheese on top. Pour remaining rice mixture in casserole and top with remaining cheese. Bake uncovered for 35 minutes or until bubbly hot. Serves 10 to 12.

Rice and Broccoli

2 tablespoons (¼ stick) butter
2 ribs celery, chopped
1 onion, finely chopped
2 cups cooked rice (use instant rice)
1 (16 ounce) package frozen chopped broccoli, thawed
1 (14 ounce) jar processed cheese spread
1 (10 ounce) can cream of chicken soup, undiluted
1 teaspoon salt

Preheat oven to 350°. Melt butter in small skillet and saute celery and onion on low heat, do not brown. In large mixing bowl combine rice, celery, onion, broccoli, cheese, soup and salt and mix well. Place in sprayed 9 x 13 x 2-inch baking dish and bake for 35 minutes. To make ahead of time, freeze before baking, thaw when ready to bake. Serves 10.

Admiral Nimitz Museum in Fredericksburg houses the Museum of the Pacific War and is dedicated to all who served during World War II.

Chili-Cheese Grits

4 packets instant grits
¼ cup (½ stick) butter, melted
¾ cup grated cheddar cheese
¾ teaspoon seasoned salt

1 (4 ounce) can chopped green chilies
1 egg, beaten

Preheat oven to 350°. Prepare grits according to directions. Add melted butter, grated cheese, seasoned salt and green chilies. Let cool 5 to 10 minutes then stir in beaten egg. Cover and bake for 35 minutes or until center is set. Serves 6.

Hagerman National Wildlife Refuge is 11,300 acres of land and water preserved for migrating and wintering waterfowl on the Big Mineral Arm of Lake Texoma.

Red Rice

1 (16 ounce) package smoked
    sausage, sliced
2 (10 ounce) cans diced tomatoes
    and green chilies

3 cups chicken broth
2 tablespoons creole seasoning
1½ cups long-grain rice

Saute sausage in Dutch oven until brown. Stir in tomatoes and green chilies, broth and seasoning and bring to boil. Stir in rice, cover, reduce heat and simmer for 25 minutes. Uncover and cook until liquid absorbs.

Texas is the first state to enter the United States as a sovereign nation. The Republic of Texas entered the U.S. in 1845, three years before California entered the U.S.

Main Dishes

Stuffed Chicken Rolls

8 boneless, skinless chicken breast
    halves
2 cups corn flake crumbs (or crispy
    rice cereal crumbs)
3 tablespoons taco seasoning mix
1 (8 ounce) package cream cheese,
    softened
1 teaspoon dried cilantro
1 teaspoon dried sweet basil

1 teaspoon dried parsley flakes
1/4 teaspoon garlic powder
1 teaspoon seasoned salt or
    summer savory
1/2 green bell pepper, finely
    chopped
2 tablespoons (1/4 stick) butter
2 cups cracker crumbs

Preheat oven to 350°. Place each chicken breast on cutting board
and pound with meat mallet until chicken is 1/4-inch thick. Mix
crumbs and taco seasoning and set aside. Place cream cheese in
bowl and add seasonings and bell pepper. Mix with fork. Place
1/8 cream cheese mixture on each chicken breast and roll up. Roll
in cracker crumbs. Melt butter in 9 x 13 x 2-inch baking dish
and place chicken rolls, edge side down in baking dish. Bake for
50 minutes. You can serve the whole breast or in 1/2-inch slices.
Serves 8.

Mexican Delight

- 6 boneless chicken breast halves
- 1 (9½ ounce) bag Mexican corn chips
- 1 onion, chopped
- 3 ribs celery, chopped
- 1 (10 ounce) can cream of chicken soup
- 2 (10 ounce) can tomatoes and green chilies
- 1 (16 ounce) package cubed Mexican processed cheese

Preheat oven to 350°. In large saucepan simmer chicken breasts in water about 30 minutes or until done. Cool and cut in small bite-size pieces. Place half bag of chips in sprayed 9 x 13 x 2-inch baking dish. Crush slightly with palm of hand. In large saucepan combine onion, celery, chicken soup, tomatoes and green chilies and cheese. Cook on medium heat and stir until cheese melts. Add chicken pieces and pour over chips. Crush remaining chips in a resealable plastic bag with rolling pin. Sprinkle over chicken-cheese mixture. Bake for 35 minutes or until bubbly around edges. Serves 8.

Cilantro Chicken

1 teaspoon seasoned salt
1 teaspoon seasoned pepper
2 teaspoons cilantro
1¼ teaspoons ground cumin, divided
8 boneless, skinless chicken breast
　　halves
2 cups cracker crumbs
Oil

3 tablespoons (⅓ stick) butter
¼ cup flour
½ teaspoon salt
1 teaspoon seasoned pepper
1 teaspoon cilantro
2 cups milk
⅓ cup dry white wine
1 cup grated Monterey Jack cheese

Preheat oven to 350°.   Mix seasoned salt, seasoned pepper, cilantro
and 1 teaspoon cumin. Sprinkle over chicken breasts and dip in
breadcrumbs. Pour a small amount of oil in large skillet and brown
chicken. Remove to 9 x 13 x 2-inch sprayed baking dish. In saucepan melt butter and blend in flour and remaining seasonings. Add
milk, stirring constantly and cook until mixture thickens. Remove
from heat and stir in wine. Pour sauce over chicken and bake for
45 minutes. Remove from oven and sprinkle cheese on top of each
piece of chicken and return to oven for 5 minutes longer. Serves 8.

Savory Oven-Fried Chicken

1 egg
½ cup milk
2 cups corn flake crumbs
1 teaspoon seasoned salt
1 teaspoon summer savory
1 teaspoon parsley flakes
1 teaspoon dehydrated minced onion
½ teaspoon black pepper
¼ teaspoon garlic powder
2 tablespoons (¼ stick) butter
8 chicken breast halves or 1 cut up chicken

Preheat oven to 325°. In small bowl beat eggs and milk. In another small bowl combine corn flake crumbs and seasonings. Melt butter in microwave in 9 x 13 x 2-inch baking dish. Dip each breast half in egg and milk mixture and coat thoroughly with seasoned crumbs. Place chicken in baking dish and bake uncovered for 55 minutes or until coating on chicken is golden brown. Serves 8.

Imperial Chicken Casserole

5 chicken breast halves, cooked, cubed
2 (8 ounce) cartons sour cream
1 (7 ounce) package ready-cut spaghetti, uncooked
2 (10 ounce) cans cream of chicken soup

1 (4 ounce) can mushroom halves, drained
½ cup (1 stick) butter, melted
⅛ teaspoon black pepper
1 cup freshly grated parmesan cheese

Preheat oven to 325°. Combine chicken, sour cream, spaghetti, chicken soup, mushrooms, butter and black pepper. Pour into sprayed 9 x 13 x 2-inch baking dish. Sprinkle cheese on top. Bake uncovered for 50 minutes. Serves 2 to 10.

Texas is the largest producer of sheep and lambs in the U.S.

Favorite Chicken

- 8 boneless, skinless chicken breast halves
- 1 (8 ounce) bottle Catalina dressing
- 1 (1 ounce) packet dry onion soup mix
- 1 (8 ounce) jar apricot preserves
- 1 tablespoon lime juice
- Cooked rice

Preheat oven to 325°. Place chicken breasts in greased 9 x 13 x 2-inch baking dish. In saucepan combine Catalina dressing, soup mix, apricot preserves and lime juice and heat just enough to mix well. Pour over chicken breasts and bake covered for 1 hour and 10 minutes. Serve over hot rice. Serves 8.

Texas is the largest producer of goats in the U.S.

Chicken a la Orange

8 boneless, skinless chicken breast
   halves
Oil
1 (1 ounce) packet onion soup mix

1 (6 ounce) can frozen orange juice
   concentrate, thawed
⅔ cup water
Cooked rice

Preheat oven to 350°. In skillet brown chicken breasts in oil. Place chicken breasts in greased 9 x 13 x 2-inch baking dish. In small bowl combine onion soup mix, orange juice and water. Stir well. (Make sure lumps of seasoning in onion soup mix are diluted and mixed.) Pour over chicken breasts. Bake covered for 40 minutes. Serve over hot rice. Serves 8.

Texas is the largest producer of wool in the U.S.

Chicken Breasts Supreme

- 1 (1 ounce) packet golden onion soup mix
- 1/3 cup chili sauce
- 1/3 cup white wine tarragon vinegar
- 2/3 cup honey
- 1/4 cup oil
- 8 boneless, skinless chicken breast halves
- 2 tablespoons cornstarch
- 1/4 cup water
- Cooked rice

Preheat oven to 350°. Place soup mix, chili sauce, vinegar, honey and oil in jar. Shake ingredients well. Place chicken breasts in single layer in sprayed 9 x 13 x 2-inch baking dish. Pour sauce over chicken and bake covered 50 minutes. When chicken is done, remove chicken breasts to a platter. Mix cornstarch and water, pour in sauce in baking dish and stir well. Place back in hot oven for 10 minutes or until sauce thickens. Serve chicken over hot rice and cover with sauce. Serves 8.

Jazzy Chicken and Dressing

1 (8 ounce) package stuffing
3 cups diced, cooked chicken
1 (15 ounce) can golden hominy,
    drained
1 (4 ounce) can chopped green
    chilies, drained
½ cup chopped red bell pepper
2 tablespoons dried parsley flakes
1 (10 ounce) can cream of chicken
    soup, undiluted

1 (8 ounce) carton sour cream
½ cup water
4 tablespoons (½ stick) butter,
    melted
2 teaspoons ground cumin
½ teaspoon salt
1 (8 ounce) package shredded
    Monterey Jack cheese

Preheat oven to 350°. In large mixing bowl combine all ingredients
except cheese. Mix well and pour into greased 9 x 13 x 2-inch
baking dish and cover with foil. Bake for 35 minutes. Uncover and
sprinkle with cheese. Bake an additional 5 minutes.

Chicken Souffle

- 16 slices white bread, buttered on one side, crusts removed
- 5 boneless, skinless chicken breast halves, cooked, sliced
- ½ cup mayonnaise
- 1 cup grated cheddar cheese, divided
- 5 eggs
- 2 cups milk
- 1 teaspoon salt
- 1 (10 ounce) can cream of mushroom soup, undiluted

Preheat oven to 350°. Spray a 9 x 13 x 2-inch glass baking dish. Line bottom with 8 slices of bread. Cover with sliced chicken, spread chicken slices with mayonnaise and sprinkle with ½ cup cheese. (You could use deli-sliced chicken instead of cooking the chicken breasts.) Top with remaining 8 slices bread. Beat eggs, milk and salt and pour over entire casserole. Chill overnight or all day. When ready to bake, spread soup over top with the back of large spoon. Bake covered for 45 minutes. Uncover and sprinkle with remaining cheddar cheese and return to oven and bake 15 minutes longer. Serves 8 to 10.

Texas Chili

3½ pounds lean ground beef
1 onion, chopped
1 (15 ounce) can tomato sauce
1 (10 ounce) can diced tomatoes and
    green chilies
5 tablespoons ground cumin

1 teaspoon oregano
2 tablespoons chili
    powder
1 tablespoon salt
2 cups water

Combine ground beef and onion in large stockpot or roasting pan and brown. Add all remaining ingredients. Bring to boil. Reduce heat and simmer for 1 hour. Serve with crackers or cornbread. Serves 8.

Confederate Air Force Flying Museum in Midland features the nation's finest and most complete collection of operational World War II combat aircraft.

Slow-Cook Brisket

4 to 6 pound trimmed brisket
Seasoned salt
Seasoned pepper

1 (1 ounce) packet onion soup mix
¼ cup worcestershire sauce

Preheat oven to 375°. Place brisket in large roasting pan or Dutch oven. Generously sprinkle with seasoned salt and seasoned pepper. Spread onion soup mix over top of brisket. Pour worcestershire sauce in the sides of pan and add 1 cup of water. Cook for 1 hour at 375° then lower oven temperature to 275° and cook 1 hour per pound. When done let brisket sit at room temperature for 30 minutes before slicing. Slice brisket and place slices in 9 x 13 x 2-inch baking dish. Pour gravy left in pan over slices. To serve cold, do not pour gravy over brisket.

Texas is the largest producer of mohair in the U.S.

Chicken-Fried Veal Steaks

½ cup milk
1 egg
¾ cup flour
½ teaspoon salt

¼ teaspoon black pepper
4 veal cutlets
Oil

In small bowl beat egg and milk. In another small flat bowl mix flour, salt and pepper. First coat each cutlet with seasoned flour then dip in milk-egg mixture and finally coat each cutlet a second time with seasoned flour. When coating cutlet with flour, press flour into cutlet so it will adhere to surface of cutlet. Deep-fry in oil. Drain on paper towel and serve hot.

Texas is the largest producer of upland cotton in the U.S.

Hot and Spicy Steak Strips

1 (10 ounce) can tomatoes and green chilies
1 onion, chopped
1 tablespoon cornstarch
¼ cup soy sauce
¼ cup sherry
1 teaspoon garlic powder
2 ribs celery, sliced
1 (4 ounce) can sliced mushrooms, drained
1 teaspoon seasoned salt
1 teaspoon black pepper
¼ teaspoon ground ginger
1 pound lean round steak, sliced in thin strips*
Cooked rice or noodles

Preheat oven to 350°. Pour tomatoes and green chilies in sprayed 3-quart casserole dish. Add onion and cornstarch and mix well. Add soy sauce, sherry, garlic powder, celery, mushrooms, seasoned salt, pepper and ginger and mix well. Stir in steak slices and cover. Bake 1 hour. Serve over white rice or noodles. Serves 8.

Round steak will slice easier if it is partially frozen.

Taco Pie

1 pound lean ground beef
½ bell pepper, chopped
½ teaspoon salt
1 (15 ounce) can Mexican seasoned
   tomatoes
1 cup water

1 tablespoon chili powder
¼ teaspoon garlic powder
1½ cups grated cheddar cheese
1 (6 ounce) package corn muffin mix
1 egg
⅔ cup milk

Preheat oven to 375°. In large skillet brown ground beef and bell pepper. Drain off fat. Add salt, tomatoes, water, chili powder and garlic powder. Cook on medium heat for 10 minutes or until most of liquid cooks out, but not dry. Pour into greased 9 x 13 x 2-inch glass baking dish. Sprinkle with cheese. Combine corn muffin mix, egg and milk and beat well. Pour on top of cheese. Bake for 25 minutes or until corn topping is light brown. Let stand about 10 minutes before serving. Serves 8.

Smothered Steak

1 to 1½ pounds round steak, tenderized
Pepper
Flour
Oil
1 (10 ounce) can golden cream of mushroom soup, undiluted

1½ (15 ounce) cans evaporated milk
1 (1 ounce) packet onion soup mix
1 (4 ounce) can sliced mushrooms with liquid

Preheat oven to 350°. Trim any fat from steak. Season with pepper. Cut steak in serving-size pieces, dip each piece in flour and coat well. Brown in large skillet with small amount of oil. Place steak pieces in sprayed 9 x 13 x 2-inch glass baking dish. In same skillet combine mushroom soup, milk and onion soup mix. Heat. Blend and pour over steak pieces. Cover with foil and bake for 1 hour. Serves 4 to 6.

Texas is the largest producer of grain sorghum in the U.S.

Mexican Casserole

Tortilla chips
1½ pounds lean ground beef
1 onion, chopped
1 bell pepper, chopped
1 (15 ounce) can Mexican seasoned
    tomatoes
1 (15 ounce) can ranch-style pinto
    beans with liquid

¼ cup picante sauce
1 (1 ounce) packet dry onion soup
    mix
1 teaspoon seasoned salt
1 teaspoon chili powder
¼ teaspoon garlic powder
½ teaspoon ground coriander
2 cups grated cheddar cheese

Preheat oven to 350°. In sprayed 9 x 13 x 2-inch baking dish, place about 40 chips on bottom of dish. Crush slightly with hands. In large skillet brown beef, onion and bell pepper. Add all ingredients except cheese and mix well. Heat and simmer 3 to 4 minutes. Spoon over chips in baking dish and cover with cheese. Cover with foil and bake for 35 minutes. Serves 10.

Ginger Beef Stir-Fry

1 to 1½ pounds top loin steak*
Pepper
Oil
1 onion, chopped
1 bell pepper, chopped
2 tablespoons lime juice
1 tablespoon sugar
2 tablespoons dry sherry
2 teaspoons soy sauce
1 teaspoon ground ginger
1 teaspoon garlic powder
1 tablespoon cornstarch
¾ cup water
Hot cooked rice

Slice steak diagonally across grain into thin strips. Sprinkle with pepper. Pour enough oil to cover bottom of large skillet or wok. Turn heat to medium high. Place steak slices in skillet and brown. Turn heat down, add onion and bell pepper and simmer 4 minutes. In small bowl combine lime juice, sugar, sherry, soy sauce, ginger, garlic powder, cornstarch and water. Pour in skillet with beef and bring to boil, stirring constantly for 4 minutes. Serve over hot rice. Serves 6.

Steak will slice easier if it is partially frozen.

Best Pot Roast

4 to 5 pound boneless rump roast
Seasoned salt
Seasoned pepper
Garlic powder
1 cup water
6 medium potatoes, peeled,
    quartered

8 carrots, peeled, quartered
2 onions, peeled, quartered
Gravy:
3 tablespoons cornstarch
¾ cup water
½ teaspoon salt

Preheat oven to 350°. Put roast in roasting pan with lid and
sprinkle liberally with salt, pepper and garlic powder. Add 1 cup
water, cover and bake 3 hours. Add potatoes, carrots and onions.
Cook another 35 to 40 minutes or until vegetables are done. Place
potatoes, carrots and onion around roast on platter. Combine
cornstarch and water and add to juices left in roaster. Add salt and
cook on high on stove top until gravy thickens, stirring constantly.
Serves 8.

Sweet and Sour Pork Loin

5 to 6 pound pork loin
1 (12 ounce) bottle chili sauce
1 (16 ounce) jar apricot preserves
Marinade:
⅔ cup soy sauce
⅔ cup oil
3 tablespoons crystallized ginger, chopped fine
2 tablespoons lime juice
1 teaspoon garlic powder

Mix marinade and place in large plastic bag. Add pork loin. Marinate 24 to 36 hours, turning several times. Preheat oven to 325°. Place pork loin and marinade in roaster and cook for 3 hours. Mix chili sauce and apricot preserves and pour over pork loin. Return to oven for 20 minutes. Allow pork loin to set for 20 minutes before slicing.

Texas had the first rodeo to give prizes in the world. It was held in Pecos, Texas with ranch hands from area ranches.

Pork Chops with Rice

6 to 8 pork chops
Salt and pepper
Flour
2 tablespoons oil
1 onion, chopped
1 bell pepper, chopped
1 jalapeno pepper, chopped, optional

¾ cup uncooked rice
1 (14 ounce) can beef broth
½ cup water
1 teaspoon seasoned salt
½ teaspoon pepper
1 (8 ounce) carton sour cream
1 cup grated cheddar cheese

Preheat oven to 350°. Season pork chops with salt and pepper and dredge in flour. Heat oil in skillet and brown pork chops on both sides. In mixing bowl combine and mix all ingredients except cheese. Pour in sprayed 9 x 13 x 2-inch baking dish. Place pork chops in rice mixture. Cover baking dish with foil and bake 50 minutes. Uncover and sprinkle with cheese on top and bake another 5 minutes. Serves 6 to 8.

Pancho Villa Stew

- 2 pounds pork loin, cut in bite-size cubes
- 2 tablespoons oil
- 1 pound smoked link sausage, cut in ½-inch slices
- 3 (14 ounce) cans chicken broth
- 1 (15 ounce) can whole tomatoes with liquid
- 3 (4 ounce) cans chopped green chilies with liquid
- 1 large onion, chopped
- 1 teaspoon garlic powder
- 2 teaspoons ground cumin
- 1 teaspoon cocoa
- 1 teaspoon dried oregano
- ½ teaspoon salt
- 2 (15 ounce) cans pinto beans with liquid
- 1 (15 ounce) can hominy with liquid
- 1 (8 ounce) can whole kernel corn with liquid
- Flour tortillas

In roasting pan brown pork cubes in oil and stir often. Add sliced sausages, chicken broth, tomatoes, green chilies, onion, garlic powder, cumin, cocoa, oregano and salt. Bring to boil, reduce heat and simmer 45 minutes. Add pinto beans, hominy and corn and bring to boil. Reduce heat and simmer another 30 minutes. Serve with buttered flour tortillas. It is also good served with cornbread. Serves 8 to 10.

Fried Catfish

8 to 10 catfish fillets
Salt
Pepper
2 cups crushed cracker crumbs

⅓ cup flour
1 cup buttermilk
Oil

Dry fish with paper towels and sprinkle with salt and pepper. In bowl mix cracker crumbs with flour. Dip fillets in buttermilk then in crumb mixture and coat well. Heat ½-inch oil in skillet. Fry fish until both sides are light brown and crisp.

Tip: To make buttermilk, measure 1 cup milk and add 2 tablespoons lemon juice or vinegar and let milk rest for about 20 minutes.

The first commercially packaged chili powder and canned chilies were produced by William Gebhardt of New Braunfels. In 1911 Gebhardt built a factory in San Antonio to supply the demand.

Oven-Fried Orange Roughy

1 to 1¼ pounds orange roughy
1½ cups cracker crumbs
½ teaspoon salt
1 teaspoon seasoned salt
1 teaspoon seasoned pepper

1 tablespoon dried parsley flakes
1 teaspoon summery savory
1 teaspoon coriander leaves
¾ cup sour cream or mayonnaise

Preheat oven to 375°. Cut orange roughy in serving-size pieces. Mix cracker crumbs and all seasonings in medium-size dish. Place a piece of sprayed foil on baking sheet or 9 x 13 x 2-inch baking dish. Dip orange roughy in sour cream or mayonnaise and then in cracker crumb mixture and coat well. Place pieces on foil and bake uncovered 20 minutes or until fish is light brown and cooked through. Serves 6.

Skillet-Shrimp Scampi

2 teaspoons olive oil
2 pounds uncooked shrimp, peeled, veined
⅔ cup herb-garlic marinade with lemon juice

¼ cup chopped green onions with tops

Heat oil in large saucepan and add shrimp and marinade. Cook, stirring often, until shrimp turns pink. Stir in green onions. Serve over hot, cooked rice or your favorite pasta.

Buffalo or the American bison is found on ranches in Texas. In the 1880's on one day in Fort Worth, more than 200,000 hides were sold. Had it not been for the efforts of Texas Ranger Col. Charles Goodnight to control hunting, the buffalo might be extinct today.

Cakes and Pies

Brown Sugar-Rum Cake

1½ cups (3 sticks) butter, softened
1 (16 ounce) package brown sugar
1 cup sugar
5 large eggs
¾ cup milk
¼ cup rum

2 teaspoons vanilla extract
3 cups flour
2 teaspoons baking powder
¼ teaspoon salt
1½ cups chopped pecans
Whipped topping

Preheat oven to 325°. With electric mixer beat butter and sugars at medium speed about 5 minutes. Add eggs, one at a time, beating just until yellow disappears. Combine milk, rum and vanilla. Combine flour, baking powder and salt. Add half flour mixture and mix. Add milk mixture and mix. Add remaining flour mixture, beating at low speed. Fold in pecans. Pour into greased, floured tube pan. Bake for 1 hour and 25 minutes or until a toothpick inserted in the center comes out clean. Cool in pan for 20 minutes, remove from pan, cool and serve with whipped topping.

Poppy-Seed Cake

2 tablespoons poppy-seeds
2 teaspoons almond extract
2 teaspoons vanilla extract
2 teaspoons butter extract
1 teaspoon rum flavoring
3 cups sugar
1 cup shortening
5 eggs
3 cups flour

¼ teaspoon baking soda
¼ teaspoon salt
1 cup buttermilk

Glaze:
2 cups powdered sugar
¼ cup orange juice
¼ teaspoon almond extract
1 teaspoon butter extract

Preheat oven to 350°. In small bowl soak poppy seed in extracts and rum flavoring. Set aside. In mixing bowl, cream sugar and shortening until light and fluffy. Add eggs, one at a time and beat well. Mix flour, baking soda and salt. Alternately add dry ingredients and buttermilk. Mix well. Add poppy seed mixture and blend well. Pour in greased, floured tube pan. Bake for 1 hour and 15 minutes or until toothpick inserted in the center comes out clean. Cool. Mix glaze ingredients, pour over cake and let it run down sides.

Pineapple Cake with Amaretto Sauce

1 cup (2 sticks) butter, softened
2 cups sugar
5 eggs
2½ cups flour
½ cup yellow cornmeal
1 teaspoon baking powder
¼ teaspoon baking soda

1 cup lemon yogurt
1 teaspoon vanilla extract
1 (15 ounce) can crushed pineapple,
    drained
1 (20 ounce) can lemon pie filling
⅔ cup amaretto
½ cup water

Preheat oven to 350°. In mixing bowl, beat butter and sugar. Add eggs one at a time. In another bowl mix flour, cornmeal, baking powder and soda. Add half flour mixture to egg mixture and beat. Add yogurt and vanilla and beat. Add the remaining flour. Fold in pineapple. Pour in greased, floured Bundt® pan. Bake for 70 minutes or until toothpick inserted near center comes out clean. Cool in pan for 15 minutes. Remove from pan and cool. For sauce, mix pie filling, amaretto and water. Serve over slices of cake.

Chocolate Pound Cake

1 cup (2 sticks) butter
1 cup shortening
3 cups sugar
5 large eggs
3 cups flour
½ cup cocoa
¾ teaspoon baking powder
½ teaspoon salt
2 teaspoons cinnamon
1 cup milk
1 teaspoon vanilla extract
Powdered sugar

Preheat oven to 350°. In mixing bowl, mix butter, shortening and sugar. Beat about 2 minutes. Add eggs, one at a time, and beat well. Add flour, cocoa, baking powder, salt and cinnamon to cream mixture alternately with milk and vanilla, beginning and ending with flour mixture. Beat after each addition. Spoon batter into greased, floured Bundt® pan, bake for 1 hour and 15 minutes or until toothpick inserted in center of cake comes out clean. Cool in pan for about 15 minutes. Remove from pan and cool. Dust cake with powdered sugar.

Piña Colada Cake

1 (18.25 ounce) package yellow
  cake mix
1 (3¾ ounce) package instant
  vanilla pudding mix
1 (15 ounce) can cream of coconut,
  divided
½ cup rum

⅓ cup oil
4 eggs
1 (8 ounce) can crushed pineapple,
  drained
Whipped topping

Preheat oven to 350°. In large mixing bowl combine cake mix,
pudding mix, ½ cup cream of coconut, rum, oil and eggs. Beat
at medium speed 2 minutes. Stir in pineapple. Pour in greased,
floured Bundt® pan. Bake 55 minutes or until toothpick inserted
near center comes out clean. Cool 15 minutes in pan and transfer
to cake plate. With table knife, poke holes about half way down
cake every 1 to 2 inches. Slowly spoon remaining cream of
coconut over cake and let mixture soak in cake. Chill. Serve each
slice with a dollup of whipped topping.

Chocolate-Glazed Almond Cheesecake

2½ cups chocolate cookie crumbs
⅓ cup butter, melted
3 (8 ounce) packages cream cheese, softened
1¼ cups sugar
3 large eggs
2 teaspoons vanilla extract
3 teaspoons almond extract
Chocolate Glaze:
1 cup whipping cream
1⅓ cups chocolate chips
1 teaspoon vanilla extract

Preheat oven to 350°. For crust, combine chocolate crumbs with melted butter and mix. Press crumbs in bottom of buttered 9-inch springform pan. In large mixing bowl beat cream cheese until smooth. Blend in sugar, eggs and extracts. Pour in crust and bake for 45 minutes. Turn oven off and allow cake to cool with door open. Refrigerate for 3 hours. In small saucepan scald cream and add chocolate, stirring until chocolate melts. Add vanilla and stir. Cool. Pour glaze over top of cheesecake and chill several hours before slicing.

Margarita Cheesecake

36 vanilla wafers, crushed
¼ cup (½ stick) butter, melted
2 (8 ounce) packages cream cheese,
    softened
¾ cup sugar
2 individual-size envelopes instant
    margarita mixes

4 large eggs
⅓ cup tequila
1½ teaspoons grated lime zest,
    divided
½ teaspoon vanilla extract
2 (8 ounce) cartons sour cream
¼ cup sugar

Preheat oven to 375°. Place crumbs in 9-inch springform pan. Add melted butter and mix. Pat down to make crust firm. Bake for 8 minutes. Set aside. Beat cream cheese with mixer until fluffy. Gradually add sugar and margarita mix and beat well. Add eggs, one at a time, beating after each addition. Stir in tequila, 1 teaspoon lime zest and vanilla. Pour in prepared pan. Bake 30 to 35 minutes until center is almost set. Cool. Combine sour cream, sugar and ½ teaspoon grated lime zest. Spread over top of cheesecake. Bake at 425° for 10 minutes. Chill.

Very Blueberry Cheesecake

- 34 vanilla wafers, crushed
- 6 tablespoons (¾ stick) butter, melted
- 1 envelope unflavored gelatin
- ¼ cup cold water
- 2 (8 ounce) packages cream cheese, softened
- 1 tablespoon lemon juice
- 1 (7 ounce) jar marshmallow creme
- ¼ cup powdered sugar
- 1 (16 ounce) can blueberries, drained
- 1 (8 ounce) carton whipped topping

Place crumbs in greased 9-inch springform pan. Pour melted butter in pan and mix well. Pat down. In saucepan soften gelatin in water. Place over low heat just until it dissolves. In mixing bowl combine cream cheese, lemon juice, marshmallow creme, powdered sugar and softened gelatin and beat until smooth. Puree blueberries in blender. Fold whipped topping and pureed blueberries into cream cheese mixture. Pour in springform pan. Chill several hours.

Dream Pie

1 (8 ounce) package cream cheese,
  softened
1 (12 ounce) can sweetened
  condensed milk
1 (1.5 ounce) package vanilla instant
  pudding mix

½ cup water
1 (8 ounce) carton whipped topping
2 (6 ounce) graham cracker crusts
1 (20 ounce) can apricot pie filling*

In mixing bowl, beat cream cheese and sweetened condensed milk
until smooth. Add pudding mix and water and mix. Chill 15 minutes.
Fold in whipped topping. Pour in 2 pie crusts and freeze. When
ready to serve, take out of freezer and place in refrigerator about
45 minutes before slicing and serving. Spoon ¼ cup of pie filling
on each slice of pie.

*You could use any pie filling.
Variation: Use 2 chocolate pie crusts. Pour 2 or 3 tablespoons
chocolate ice cream topping over pie. Top with chocolate
shavings.

Creamy Lemon Pie

1 (8 ounce) package cream cheese, softened
1 (12 ounce) can sweetened condensed milk
¼ cup lemon juice
1 (20 ounce) can lemon pie filling
1 (9 inch) graham cracker crust

Cream cheese with mixer. Add sweetened condensed milk and lemon juice. Beat until mixture is creamy. Fold in lemon pie filling and stir well. Pour in piecrust. Chill several hours before slicing and serving.

Because Texas is on the migratory path between North, Central and South America for many species of birds, it has become a world-class bird-watching destination. The World Birding Center in the Lower Rio Grande Valley protects wildlife habitat and offers educational centers and observation sites for more than 450 species of birds.

Pumpkin-Chiffon Pie

1 envelope unflavored gelatin
¼ cup cold water
3 eggs
1 cup sugar, divided
1¼ cups pumpkin
⅔ cup milk

½ teaspoon ginger
½ teaspoon nutmeg
½ teaspoon cinnamon
½ teaspoon salt
1 baked crust

Soften gelatin in cold water. Set aside. Separate eggs and set whites aside. Beat yolks slightly and add ½ cup sugar, pumpkin, milk, spices and salt. Cook in double boiler until custard consistency, stirring constantly. Mix in softened gelatin and dissolve in hot custard. Cool. Beat egg whites, gradually adding the other ½ cup sugar. Fold in stiffly beaten egg whites into cooled pumpkin mixture. Pour into crust. Chill several hours before slicing.

Caramel-Apple Pie

18 caramel candies
¼ cup milk
1 (10-inch) deep-dish baked crust
1 cup walnuts or pecans, divided
1 (8 ounce) package cream cheese, softened
1½ cups powdered sugar
¾ (8 ounce) carton whipped topping
1 (20 ounce) can apple pie filling

In saucepan melt caramels with milk, stirring constantly. Pour in bottom of baked pie crust. Sprinkle with ¾ cup nuts. Cool. In mixing bowl, whip cream cheese and powdered sugar until smooth and creamy. Fold in whipped topping and pour over caramels and nuts. Refrigerate about and hour. Pour apple pie filling over cream cheese mixture. Sprinkle remaining nuts over pie filling. Chill overnight or at least several hours before slicing.

Blueberry Crumble

1 (13 ounce) package wild
   blueberry muffin mix
2/3 cup sugar, divided
1/2 teaspoon cinnamon
1/2 cup (1 stick) butter, melted

2/3 cup chopped pecans
1 (16 ounce) can blueberry pie
   filling
1 teaspoon cinnamon

Preheat oven to 350°. In bowl combine muffin mix, 1/3 cup sugar, cinnamon and melted butter. Mix until crumbly. Add pecans and mix and set aside. Pour blueberry pie filling in sprayed 9 x 13 x 2-inch glass baking dish. Pour can undrained blueberries that comes in the mix over top of pie filling. Sprinkle remaining sugar mixed with cinnamon over top. Crumble with your hands and sprinkle muffin mixture over the top of the pie filling. Bake for 35 minutes. To serve, hot or room temperature, top with a dip of vanilla ice cream. Serves 8.

Fruit Fajitas

1 (20 ounce) can cherry pie filling*
10 small flour tortillas
2 cups water

1½ cups sugar
¾ cup (1½ sticks) butter
1 teaspoon almond extract

Preheat oven to 350°. Divide pie filling equally on flour tortillas. Roll up and place in sprayed 9 x 13 x 2-inch baking dish. In saucepan mix water, sugar and butter and bring to boil. Add almond extract and pour over flour tortillas. Place in refrigerator and let stand 1 to 24 hours. Bake for 20 to 25 minutes until brown and bubbly. Serve hot or room temperature with spoonful of whipped topping. Serves 8.

Other pie filling may be used in place of cherry pie filling.

Dixie Pie

24 large marshmallows
1 cup evaporate milk
1 (8 ounce) carton whipping cream,
    whipped

3 tablespoons bourbon
1 (9 inch) prepared chocolate
    piecrust

Melt marshmallows and milk in saucepan, stirring constantly. Do
not boil. Cool in refrigerator. Fold in whipped cream while adding
bourbon. Pour into piecrust and chill at least 5 hours before serving.

Sunny Lime Pie

2 (6 ounce) Cartons key lime pie
    yogurt
1 (3 ounce) package dry lime gelatin

1 (8 ounce) carton whipped topping
1 (9 inch) graham cracker piecrust

Combine yogurt and lime gelatin and mix well. Fold in whipped
topping. Spread in piecrust and freeze. Remove from freezer
20 minutes before slicing.

Cookies and Bars

Orange-Dream Cookies

1 cup (2 sticks) butter, softened
¾ cup sugar
½ cup firmly packed light brown
　　sugar
1 egg
2 tablespoons orange juice

2 tablespoons orange zest
2¼ cups flour
¾ teaspoon baking soda
½ teaspoon salt
1 (12 ounce) package white
　　chocolate morsels

Preheat oven to 350°. Combine butter, sugars, egg and orange juice and beat well. Add orange zest, flour, baking soda and salt and mix well. Add the white chocolate morsels and mix well. Drop dough by rounded tablespoonfuls onto ungreased baking sheets. Bake for about 12 minutes or until edges are light golden brown. Let stand on cookie sheet for about 2 minutes before removing cookies. Cool before storing.

Peanut-Butterscotch Cookies

- ½ cup (1 stick) butter, softened
- ½ cup crunchy peanut butter
- ½ cup sugar
- ¾ cup firmly packed light brown sugar
- 1 egg
- 1 teaspoon vanilla extract
- 1 tablespoon milk
- 1¾ cups flour
- ½ teaspoon baking soda
- ½ teaspoon salt
- 1 (6 ounce) package butterscotch chips

Preheat oven to 350°. Cream butter, peanut butter, sugars, egg, vanilla and milk and beat well. Add flour, baking soda and salt and mix well. Stir in butterscotch chips. Bake for about 12 minutes or until edges are light brown. Remove from oven and let stand 2 or 3 minutes before removing cookies. Cool before storing.

Aquarena Springs in San Marcos offers a unique view of the San Marcos River and its inhabitants.

Chocolate Chip Deluxe Cookies

1 cup (2 sticks) butter, softened
½ cup firmly packed brown sugar
1 cup sugar
1 egg
1 teaspoon vanilla extract
1 teaspoon baking soda
½ teaspoon salt

2¼ cups flour
½ cup flaked coconut
1 (12 ounce) package chocolate
   chips
½ cup chopped pecans
1 cup crispy rice cereal

Preheat oven to 350°. Cream butter, sugars, egg and vanilla and beat well. Add soda, salt and flour and mix well. Stir in coconut, chocolate chips, pecans and cereal and mix well. Drop by tablespoonfuls onto cookie sheet. Bake about 13 minutes or until light brown. Cool before storing.

Corpus Christi Del La Isleta in El Paso is Texas' oldest mission dating from 1681.

Cashew Cookies

1 cup (2 sticks) butter, softened
1 cup sugar
¾ cup firmly packed light brown sugar
1 egg

2⅓ cups flour
¾ teaspoon baking soda
1 teaspoon vanilla extract
1 teaspoon almond extract
1 cup chopped cashews

Preheat oven to 350°. Cream butter with sugars, add egg and beat well. Blend in flour and soda and add extracts and cashews. Mix thoroughly. Drop by teaspoonfuls onto ungreased cookie sheet. Bake for 12 to 14 minutes or until golden brown.

Texas is the largest producer of cattle and calves in the U.S.

Apricot-Angel Brownies

2 (2 ounce) bars white baking
   chocolate
1/3 cup butter
2/3 cup sugar
2 eggs, beaten
1/2 teaspoon vanilla extract
3/4 cup flour

1/2 teaspoon baking powder
1/4 teaspoon salt
1 cup finely chopped dried apricots
1 (2 ounce) package sliced almonds
1/4 cup flaked coconut

Preheat oven to 350°. Melt chocolate and butter over low heat, stirring constantly until it melts. Remove from heat and stir in sugar, eggs and vanilla and set aside. In bowl combine flour, baking powder and salt. Stir in chocolate mixture. Combine apricots, almonds and coconut and stir about 2/3 into batter. Pour into a sprayed 7 x 11 x 2-inch baking pan. Sprinkle remaining apricot mixture on top. Bake for 25 minutes or until golden brown. Cool before storing.

Death by Chocolate

1 cup (2 sticks) butter, softened
2 cups sugar
1 tablespoon vanilla extract
4 eggs
1½ cups flour
½ cup cocoa
1½ cups chopped pecans

1 (8 ounce) jar marshmallow creme
Icing:
½ cup (1 stick) butter, melted
2 tablespoons milk
3 tablespoons cocoa
3 cups powdered sugar

Preheat oven to 350°. Combine butter, sugar, vanilla and eggs. Beat 3 minutes. Add flour and cocoa and beat until thoroughly mixed. Stir in pecans. Pour into greased and floured 9 x 13 x 2-inch baking pan. Bake for 40 minutes or until toothpick inserted near center comes out clean. Immediately spread marshmallow creme over hot cake and cool. For icing, combine butter, milk, cocoa and powdered sugar. Mix well and spread over marshmallow creme.

Apricot-Almond Bars

1 (18.25 ounce) package yellow
    cake mix
½ cup (1 stick) butter, melted
½ cup finely chopped almonds
1 (12 ounce) jar apricot preserves,
    divided
1 (8 ounce) package cream cheese,
    softened

¼ cup sugar
2 tablespoons flour
⅛ teaspoon salt
1 egg
1 teaspoon vanilla extract
⅔ cup flaked coconut

Preheat oven to 350°. In large bowl, combine cake mix and butter
and mix by hand just until crumbly. Stir in almonds and reserve
1 cup crumb mixture. Lightly press remaining crumb mixture into
a sprayed 9 x 13 x 2-inch-baking pan. Carefully spread 1 cup of
preserves over crumb mixture, leaving a ¼-inch border. Beat cream
cheese in mixer until smooth and add remaining preserves, sugar, flour,
salt, egg and vanilla and beat well. Carefully spread cream cheese
mixture over top of preserves. Combine 1 cup reserved crumb mixture
and coconut and mix well. Sprinkle over cream cheese mixture. Bake
for 35 minutes or until center sets. Cool. Store in refrigerator.

Praline Squares

1½ cups flour
½ cup powdered sugar
1 cup (2 sticks) butter, divided
3½ cups chopped pecans, divided
1¼ cups corn syrup

1 cup firmly packed brown sugar
4 eggs
1 teaspoon vanilla extract
1 (10 ounce) package butterscotch chips

Preheat oven to 325°. For crust, stir flour and powdered sugar. Cut in ¾ cup (1½ sticks) butter. Stir in 1½ cups pecans. Press into greased 9 x 13 x 2-inch baking pan. Bake for 20 minutes. In medium saucepan combine syrup, brown sugar and ¼ cup (½ stick) butter. Bring to boiling point, stirring constantly. Remove from heat and cool slightly. Beat eggs with electric mixer on low speed. Continue beating, slowly adding warm mixture. Stir in 2 cups pecans and vanilla. Pour filling into crust. Sprinkle with butterscotch chips. Bake at 350° for 35 minutes or until center sets. Cool.

Peanut Clusters

1 (24 ounce) package almond bark
1 (12 ounce) package milk chocolate
   chips

5 cups salted peanuts

Melt almond bark and chocolate chips in double boiler. Stir in peanuts and mix well. Drop by tablespoonfuls on wax paper. Store in airtight container.

Roasted Mixed Nuts

1 pound mixed nuts
¼ cup maple syrup
2 tablespoons brown sugar

1 envelope ranch-style salad
   dressing mix

Combine nuts and maple syrup and mix well. Sprinkle with brown sugar and dressing. Mix and stir to gently coat nuts. Spread in greased 10 x15-inch baking pan. Bake at 300° for 25 minutes or until light brown. Cool and serve.

Index

Angel Salad 48
Apricot Angel Brownies 116
Apricot-Almond Bars 118
Apples, Treasure-Filled 30
APPETIZERS
    Crab-Dip Kick 16
    Deviled Egg Spread 14
    Deviled Ham and Cheese Spread 13
    Great Balls of Fire 12
    Green Eyes 15
    Original Hot Cheese 7
    Party Sausages 15
    Quick Trick 12
    Shrimp Boat Dip 6
    Snappy Chili Dip 9
    Super Spinach Dip 10
    Vegetable Dip
    Zippy Cheese Dip 8
Apricot Angel Brownies 116
Apricot-Almond Bars 118
Baked Cauliflower 50
BARS AND SQUARES
    Apricot Angel Brownies 116
    Apricot-Almond Bars 118
    Death By Chocolate 117
    Praline Squares 119

BEEF
    Best Pot Roast 88
    Chicken Fried Veal Steaks 82
    Ginger Beef Stir-Fry 87
    Hot and Spicy Steak Strips 83
    Mexican Casserole 86
    Slow Cook Brisket 81
    Smothered Steak 85
    Taco Pie 84
    Texas Chili 80
Best Bran Muffins 28
Best Pot Roast 88
Biscuits and Sausage Gravy 20
Black-Eyed Pea Salad 38
Blueberry Crumble 108
BREADS
    Best Bran Muffins 28
    Biscuits and Sausage Gravy 20
    Brunch Biscuits 19
    Cheese Bread 23
    Cornbread 22
    Light and Crispy Waffles 21
    Maple Spice Muffins 27
    Monterey Toast 18
Breakfast Bake 26
Broccoli Supreme 58

Brown Sugar-Rum Cake 96
Brunch Biscuits 19
BRUNCH
    Breakfast Bake 26
    Grand Kid's Special 29
    Quesadilla Pie 25
    Quick Quiche 24
CAKES
    Brown Sugar-Rum Cake 96
    Chocolate Pound Cake 99
    Pina Colada Cake 100
    Pineapple Cake with Amaretto Sauce 98
    Poppy Seed Cake 97
    Carmel Apple Pie 107
    Cashew Cookies 115
    Cauliflower Salad 36
    Cheddar Potato Casserole 62
    Cheese Bread 23
CHEESECAKES
    Chocolate Glazed Almond Cheesecake 101
    Margarita Cheesecake 102
    Very Blueberry Cheesecake 103
Cherry Cranberry Salad 41
CHICKEN
    Chicken A'la Orange 76
    Chicken Breasts Supreme 77

    Chicken Souffle 79
    Cilantro Chicken 72
    Dorito Delight 71
    Favorite Chicken 75
    Imperial Chicken Casserole 74
    Jazzy Chicken and Dressing 78
    Savory Oven Fried Chicken 73
    Stuffed Chicken Rolls 70
Chili Cheese Grits 67
Chocolate Chip Deluxe Cookies 114
Chocolate Glazed Almond Cheesecake 101
Chocolate Pound Cake 99
Cilantro Chicken 72
COOKIES
    Cashew Cookies, 115
    Chocolate Chip Deluxe Cookies 114
    Orange Dream Cookies 112
    Peanut Butterscotch Cookies 113
Cornbread 22
Cornbread Salad 39
Crap-Dip Kick 16
Cream of Zucchini Soup 34
Creamy Fruit Salad 43
Creamy Lemon Pie 105
Creamy Squash 52
Cucumbers In Sour Cream 41

Death By Chocolate 117
DESSERTS
- Apricot Angel Brownies 116
- Apricot-Almond Bars 118
- Blueberry Crumble 108
- Brown Sugar-Rum Cake 96
- Carmel Apple Pie 107
- Cashew Cookies 115
- Chocolate Chip Deluxe Cookies 114
- Chocolate Glazed Almond Cheesecake 101
- Chocolate Pound Cake 99
- Creamy Lemon Pie 105
- Death By Chocolate 117
- Dixie Pie 110
- Dream Pie 104
- Fruit Fajitas 109
- Margarita Cheesecake 102
- Orange Dream Cookies 112
- Pina Colada Cake 100
- Pineapple Cake with Amaretto Sauce 98
- Poppy Seed Cake 97
- Praline Squares 119
- Pumpkin Chiffon Cake 106
- Very Blueberry Cheesecake 103

Deviled Egg Spread 14
Deviled Ham and Cheese Spread 13
Dixie Pie 110
Dream Pie 104
Favorite Chicken 75
FISH
- Fried Catfish 92
- Oven Fried Orange Roughy 93
- Fried Catfish 92

Fruit Fajitas 109
Ginger Beef Stir-Fry 87
Ginger Shrimp Pasta Salad 47
Grand Kid's Special 29
Great Balls of Fire 12
Green Eyes 15
Hot and Spicy Steak Strips 83
Imperial Chicken Casserole 74
Incredible Broccoli Cheese Soup 32
Incredible Strawberry Salad 45
Jalapeno Green Beans 56
Jazzy Chicken and Dressing 78
Light and Crispy Waffles 21
MAIN DISHES
- Best Pot Roast 88
- Chicken a'la Orange 76
- Chicken Breasts Supreme 77
- Chicken Fried Veal Steaks 82
- Chicken Souffle 79

Cilantro Chicken 72
Dorito Delight 71
Favorite Chicken 75
Fried Catfish 92
Ginger Beef Stir-Fry 87
Hot and Spicy Steak Strips 83
Imperial Chicken Casserole 74
Jazzy Chicken and Dressing 78
Mexican Casserole 86
Oven Fried Orange Roughy 93
Pancho Villa Stew 91
Pork Chops with Rice 90
Savory Oven Fried Chicken 73
Slow Cooked Brisket 81
Smothered Steak 85
Stuffed Chicken Rolls 70
Sweet and Sour Pork Loin 89
Taco Pie 84
Texas Chili 80
Maple Spice Muffins 27
Margarita Cheesecake 102
Mashed Potatoes 61
Mexican Casserole 86
Mexican Delight 71
Mexican Mac 59
Monterey Toast 18

Orange Dream Cookies 112
Orange Fluff Salad 44
Original Hot Cheese 7
Oven Fried Orange Roughy 93
Pancho Villa Stew 91
Party Sausages 15
Peanut Butterscotch Cookies 113
Peanut Clusters 120
PIES
Carmel Apple Pie 107
Creamy Lemon Pie 105
Dixie Pie 110
Dream Pie 104
Pumpkin Chiffon Pie 106
Sunny Lime Pie 110
Pina Colada Cake 100
Pina Colada Salad 42
Pineapple Cake with Amaretto Sauce 98
Poppy Seed Cake 97
PORK
Pancho Villa Stew 91
Pork Chops with Rice 90
Sweet and Sour Pork Loin 89
Posh Squash 52
Praline Squares 119
Pumpkin Chiffon Pie 106

Quesadilla Pie 25
Quick Quiche 24
Quick Tricks 12
Ranch Beans 60
Red Rice 68
Rice and Broccoli 66
Roasted Mixed Nuts 120
SALADS
- Angel Salad 48
- Black-Eyed Pea Salad 38
- Cauliflower Salad 36
- Cherry Cranberry Salad 41
- Cornbread Salad 39
- Creamy Fruit Salad 43
- Crunchy Broccoli Salad 37
- Cucumbers In Sour Cream 41
- Ginger Shrimp Pasta Salad 47
- Incredible Strawberry Salad 45
- Orange Fluff Salad 44
- Pina Colada Salad 42
- Shrimp and English Pea Salad 46
- Waldorf Salad Supreme 40

Savory Oven Fried Chicken 73
Scalloped Corn and Tomatoes 57
Scalloped Potatoes 63
Shoe-Peg Corn 54

SHRIMP
- Ginger Shrimp Pasta Salad 47
- Shrimp and English Pea Salad 46
- Shrimp Boat Dip 6
- Skillet-Shrimp Scampi 94

SIDE DISHES
- Cheddar Potato Casserole 62
- Mashed Potatoes 61
- Red Rice 68
- Rice and Broccoli 66
- Scalloped Potatoes 63

Slow Cooked Brisket 81
Smothered Steak 85
Snappy Chili Dip 9

SOUPS
- Cream of Zucchini Soup 34
- Incredible Broccoli Cheese Soup 32
- Taco Soup 33
- White Lightning Chili 35

Spinach Special 55

SQUASH
- Creamy Squash 52
- Posh Squash 52
- Squash Dressing 53
- Zippy Zucchini 51

Stuffed Chicken Rolls 70

Sunny Lime Pie 110
Super Spinach Dip 10
Sweet and Sour Pork Loin 89
Sweet Potato Casserole 64
Taco Pie 84
Taco Soup 33
Texas Chili 80
Texas Rice 65
Treasure-Filled Apples 30
Vegetable Dip 11
VEGETABLES
    Baked Cauliflower 50
    Black-Eyed Pea Salad 38
    Broccoli Supreme 58
    Cauliflower Salad 36
    Cheddar Potato Casserole 62
    Chili Cheese Grits 67
    Creamy Squash 52
    Crunchy Broccoli Salad 37
    Jalapeno Green Beans 56
    Mashed Potatoes 61
    Mexican Mac 59
    Posh Squash 52
    Ranch Beans 60
    Rice and Broccoli 66
    Scalloped Corn and Tomatoes 57

Scalloped Potatoes 63
Shoe Peg Corn 54
Spinach Special 55
Squash Dressing 53
Sweet Potato Casserole 64
Texas Rice 65
Zippy Zucchini 51
Very Blueberry Cheesecake 103
Walforf Salad Supreme 40
White Lightning Chili 35
Zippy Cheese Dip 8
Zippy Zucchini 51

COOKBOOKS PUBLISHED BY COOKBOOK RESOURCES, LLC

- The Ultimate Cooking With 4 Ingredients
- 4 Ingredient Recipes And 30-Minute Meals
- Easy Cooking With 5 Ingredients
- The Best of Cooking With 3 Ingredients
- Easy Gourmet-Style Cooking With 5 Ingredients
- Gourmet Cooking With 5 Ingredients
- Healthy Cooking With 4 Ingredients
- Easy Dessert Cooking With 5 Ingredients
- Easy Slow-Cooker Cooking
- Quick Fixes With Mixes
- Casseroles To The Rescue
- Kitchen Keepsakes/More Kitchen Keepsakes
- Mother's Recipes
- Recipe Keepsakes
- Cookie Dough Secrets
- Gifts For The Cookie Jar
- Brownies In A Jar
- 101 Brownies
- Cookie Jar Magic
- Quilters' Cooking Companion
- Classic Southern Cooking
- Classic Tex-Mex and Texas Cooking
- Classic Southwest Cooking
- Classic Pennsylvania-Dutch Cooking
- The Great Canadian Cookbook
- The Best of Lone Star Legacy Cookbook
- Lone Star Legacy
- Lone Star Legacy II
- Cookbook 25 Years
- Pass The Plate
- Authorized Texas Ranger Cookbook
- Texas Longhorn Cookbook
- Trophy Hunters' Guide To Cooking
- Mealtimes and Memories
- Holiday Recipes
- Homecoming
- Little Taste of Texas
- Little Taste of Texas II
- Texas Peppers
- Southwest Sizzler
- Southwest Ole
- Class Treats
- Leaving Home

cookbook resources LLC
Bringing Family And Friends To The Table

To Order *Little Taste of Texas II*:

Please send_____copies @ $6.95 (U.S.) each $_____

Plus postage/handling @ $2.25 each $_____

Texas residents add sales tax @ $.54 each $_____

Check or Credit Card (Canada-credit card only) **Total** $_____

Charge to my ❑ MasterCard or ❑ VISA

Account #_____

Expiration Date_____

Signature_____

Mail or Call:
Cookbook Resources
541 Doubletree Dr.
Highland Village, Texas 75077
Toll Free (866) 229-2665
(972) 317-6404 Fax

Name_____

Address_____

City_____State_____Zip_____

Phone (day)_____(night)_____